Outlaw Pete

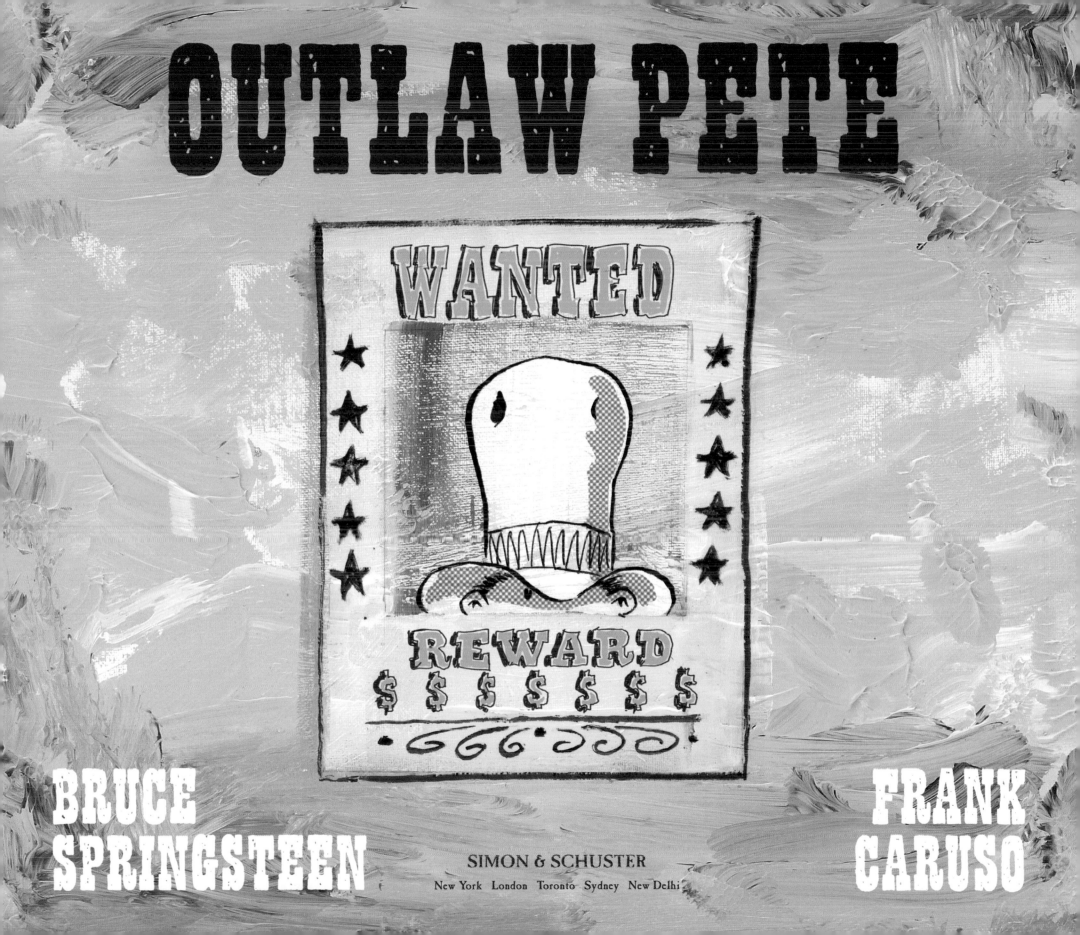

SIMON & SCHUSTER
1230 Avenue of the Americas
New York, NY 10020

First Simon & Schuster hardcover edition November 2014

SIMON & SCHUSTER and colophon are registered trademarks of Simon & Schuster, Inc.

For information about special discounts for bulk purchases,
please contact Simon & Schuster Special Sales at 1-866-506-1949 or business@simonandschuster.com

The Simon & Schuster Speakers Bureau can bring authors to your live event. For more information or to book an event
contact the Simon & Schuster Speakers Bureau at 1-866-248-3049 or visit our website at www.simonspeakers.com.

Book design by Jeff Schulz/Menagerie Co.
Creative Production: Noelle Schloendorn

Manufactured in the United States of America

10 9 8 7 6 5 4 3 2 1

Library of Congress Cataloging-in-Publication Data is available.

ISBN 978-1-5011-0385-8
ISBN 978-1-5011-0386-5 (ebook)

To Patti, Evan, Jess, Sam and Adele Springsteen —Bruce

For Laurie, Skyler and Noah —Frank

He was born a little baby
on the Appalachian Trail

At six months old he'd done
three months in jail

He robbed a bank in his diapers

and his little bare baby feet

All he said was

"Folks, my name is Outlaw Pete."

I'M OUTLAW PETE!
I'M OUTLAW PETE!
CAN YOU HEAR ME?

At twenty-five
a Mustang pony
he did steal

And he rode her 'round and
'round on heaven's wheel

Father Jesus,
I'm an outlaw,
killer and
a thief

And I slow down
only to sow my grief

He cut his trail of tears across the countryside

And where he went, women wept and men died

One night he awoke
from a vision of
his own death

Saddled his pony
and rode out deep
into the West

Married a Navajo girl
and settled down
on the res

And as the snow fell
he held their beautiful
daughter to his chest

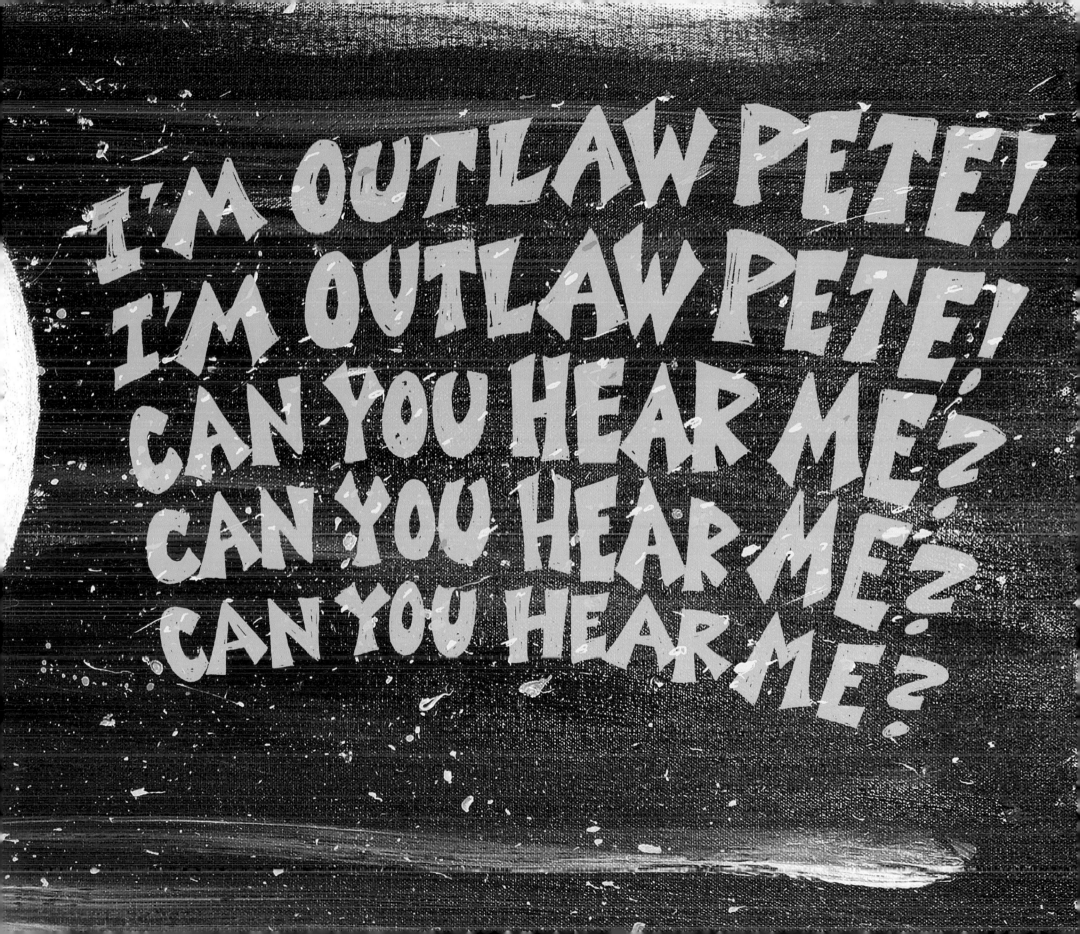

Out of the East
on an Irish stallion
came Bounty Hunter Dan

His heart quickened
and burdened by the need
to get his man

He found Pete
peacefully fishing
by the river,
pulled his gun
and got the drop

He cocked his pistol,
pulled the trigger and
shouted, "Let it start."

Pete drew a knife from his boot,
threw it, and pierced Dan through
the heart

Dan smiled as he lay in his
own blood, dying in the sun

And whispered in Pete's ear,

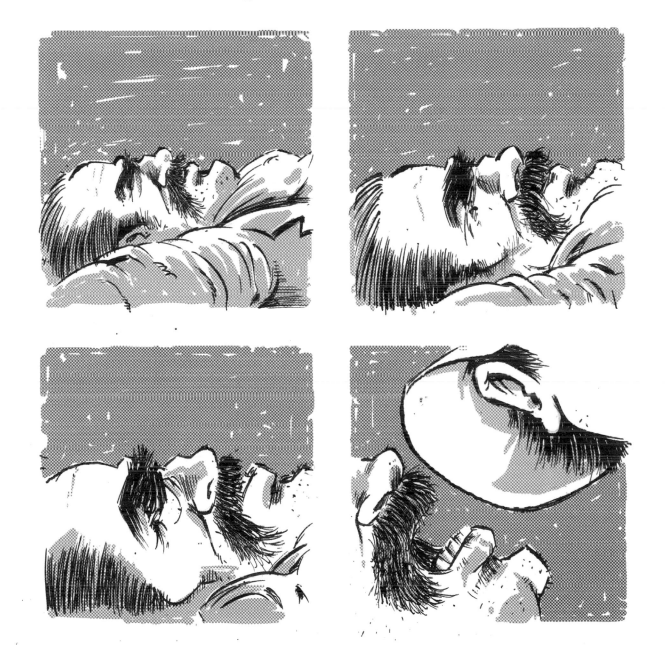

"We cannot undo these things we've done."

For forty days and nights

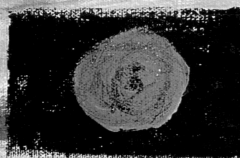

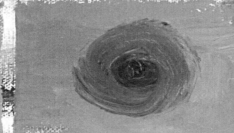

Pete rode and
did not stop

Till he sat high upon
an icy mountaintop

He watched a hawk
on a desert updraft
slip and slide

Moved to the edge
and dug his spurs
deep into his pony's side

Some say Pete and his pony
vanished over the edge

And some say
they remain frozen
high upon
that icy ledge

A young Navajo girl washes
in the river, her skin so fair

And braids a piece of
Pete's buckskin chaps
into her hair

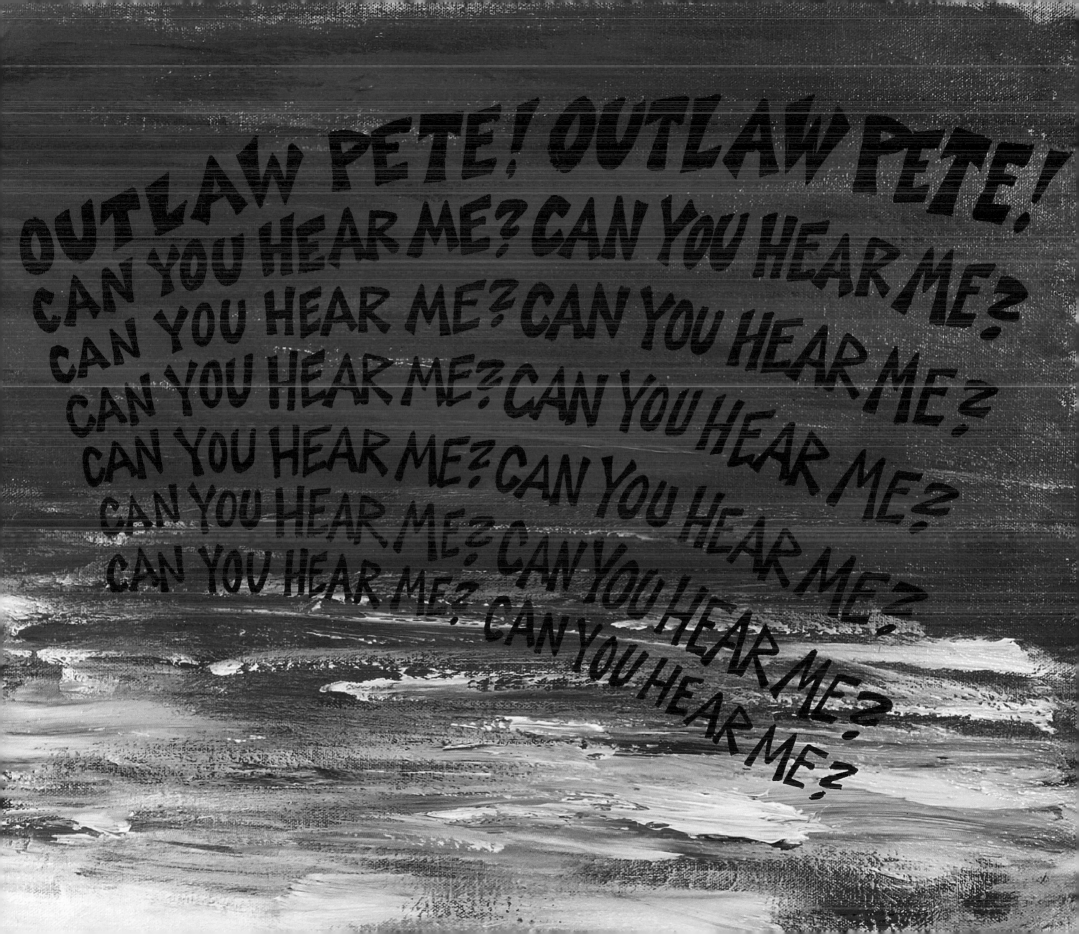

Can You Hear Me —

AFTERWORD

The story of *Outlaw Pete* flows from many sources. The wild, colorful characters of my second record, *The E Street Shuffle*, every western (spaghetti or otherwise) I've seen since I was a kid, and probably all the way back to the bedtime story *Brave Cowboy Bill* my mom used to recite from memory to me as a child.

Outlaw Pete is essentially the story of a man trying to outlive and outlast his sins. He's challenging fate by trying to outrun his poisons, his toxicity. Of course, you can't do that. Where we go, they go. You can only learn to live with it. How well or poorly we do that gauges how much grace we can bring into our lives along with our level of fortitude in body and soul.

It's not easy and I'm not sure this is a children's book, though I believe children instinctively understand passion and tragedy. And, a six-month-old, bank-robbing baby is a pretty good protagonist.

I want to thank Frank Caruso for bringing this book to me and for his wonderful art. Working with him was a pleasure. I also want to thank you, the reader . . . and wish you well as you ride.

—Bruce Springsteen